THE GRACE EMPOWERED SERIES

TRANSFORMED BY GRACE

Finding Our Identity in the Abundant
Grace of God

STEVE & SALLY WILSON

The Grace Empowered Series: Transformed by Grace, Finding our Identity in the Abundant Grace of God, by Steve and Sally Wilson © Copyright 2019 Steve and Sally Wilson. All rights reserved.

Editing and cover design by Farley Lewis.

No part of this book may be reproduced, stored or transmitted in any form or by any means, electronic or mechanical, including photocopying and recording, or by any information storage or retrieval system, except as may be expressly permitted in writing by the publisher. Requests for permission should be addressed in writing to:

Steve & Sally Publishing

2157 N Prospect Ave, Springfield MO 65803

For more information on how to order this book or any of the other materials published by Steve and Sally Wilson, contact us directly or visit our website: steveandsally.org.

Unless otherwise indicated, all scripture taken from the New American Standard Bible®, Copyright ©1960, 1962, 1963, 1968, 1971, 1972, 1973, 1975, 1977, 1995 by The Lockman Foundation. Used by permission. (www.lockman.org)

Scripture quotations marked (NLT) are taken from the Holy Bible, New Living Translation, copyright ©1996, 2004, 2015 by Tyndale House Foundation. Used by permission of Tyndale House Publishers, Inc., Carol Stream, Illinois 60188. All rights reserved.

Scripture quotations marked (NIV) are taken from the Holy Bible, NEW INTERNATIONAL VERSION®, NIV® Copyright © 1973, 1978, 1984, 2011 by Biblica, Inc.® Used by permission. All rights reserved worldwide.

Scripture quotations marked (AMP) are taken from the Amplified Bible, Copyright © 1954, 1958, 1962, 1964, 1965, 1987 by The Lockman Foundation. Used by permission.

ISBN: 979-8-61596-896-9

Contents

Introduction 9

Section 1 | Grace and Righteousness 15

Section 2 | Grace and Identity 31

Section 3 | Grace Empowered Holiness 47

Section 4 | The Spirit of Grace 63

Introduction

Our view of God affects the way we read scripture. If we see him primarily as a righteous judge, we will read it with that view; if on the other hand we see him as a loving father full of goodness, we will arrive at a different conclusion. The idea of grace is a concept profoundly affected by our understanding of God's nature. When we hear the word grace through the lens of God as judge we hear grace as rescue. However, when we read the word grace through the lens of His goodness we see it as divine empowerment that enables us to become what He destined us to be. While there is a wonderful truth in the rescue paradigm, grace is so much more than a covering for sin or a ticket to heaven.

A few years ago we had a man leave our church mad at God and mad at us. A few weeks later Farley, one of our pastors, visited him in a motel room, and found him drinking and in a foul mood. As soon as he saw Farley, the man began cursing God and us. He blamed God and the church for all of his troubles. Farley knew there was nothing much he could say to change his mind, but after the man had calmed down a little, Farley asked if he could pray for him. The man had lost his job in part because of an injury to his rotator cuff that had been torn in three places - the injury that helped convince him that God was against him. The moment Farley prayed, God healed his shoulder.

When he left the room a little while later Farley was in tears and remembers saying to himself, "God, I don't think I know You very well - a man cusses at You, and Your response is to heal him." Through circumstances like these we've come to know the goodness of God and found the revelation of grace He demonstrated to the man incredibly liberating. A few weeks later the guy showed back up at Dayspring with a big smile on his face. God's grace really has redemptive power.

God's grace has enormous transforming potential, which is exactly why the enemy does not want us to understand or access the grace of God. He knows that if we understand it correctly, we become a danger to him. He will always attempt to make us believe the wrong things and try to convince us that God is angry with us. The enemy loves to use condemnation, knowing that if our hearts condemn us, we will lack confidence. Now we know that grace is not an

INTRODUCTION

excuse for bad behavior; that is a distortion of the truth. But if the tempter can keep us feeling guilty even after we've been forgiven, he will keep us powerless.

The truth is that once we have accepted Jesus as our Savior, God already sees us as sons and daughters accepted into His family; He sees us through the finished work of Christ. We can't buy it; we can't be good enough to deserve it - it is by grace.

So what is it that we need to understand about grace? Grace is the unearned power of God at work in us changing us into the image of Jesus. Grace is not the same as mercy nor is it forgiveness. Rather, grace is the unmerited empowerment to be transformed into a new creation. Grace operates through the sanctifying work of the Holy Spirit in which spiritual life is given to us. God's grace brings our nature under the dominion of righteousness and sustains us there with an unbroken and immense supply of grace.

Faith is what brings us into grace and grace is what causes our faith grow. When we understand that we walk in His grace there is a tremendous faith released in us because we know our identity. We understand that as sons and daughters we're walking in His favor, and so acting in faith from this awareness of His approval comes naturally. The challenge for anyone who hungers for more is this: Will we put our trust solely in His grace or will we be tempted to mix in a little self-effort? The fear that often hides behind the temptation to add works to grace has to do with a desire to stay in balance.

The truth is, if we are ever to move forward, we must get over our fear of being out of balance. Think for a moment about walking. When we lift a foot to take a step we are temporarily out of balance, literally falling until we plant our foot again. To remain in perfect balance is to make a decision to never move. Too often we use the idea of staying in balance to justify the temptation to add in a little self-effort. But instead we need to trust the Holy Spirit to keep us moving in the right direction and give ourselves fully to the transforming power of grace.

Over the last few years one of the choruses we hear the church sing is about breaking every chain. The song has great imagery and accurately depicts the process of breaking free from history and bondage and into the fullness of all God has for us. As we sing this, thoughts will come into our minds about what those chains are and often there is a specific call given to shake off anything that would hold us back.

We have heard these chains itemized as sin, fear, condemnation, addiction, physical and mental illness and a host of other spiritual maladies. But not once have we heard anyone call for the chain of self-effort to be broken, and yet it is one of the greatest hindrances to the operation of the grace of God in our lives.

INTRODUCTION

One of the cautions the apostle Paul set for himself is that he wanted his righteousness to come by faith and not by his ability to keep the law (Phil 3:9). With all of his knowledge and discipline he recognized how easy it would be to slip back into performance and miss the transforming power of grace. Our identity must be fixed securely in Christ's righteousness that has been offered to us as a free gift of grace.

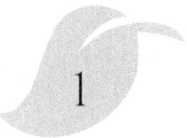

1

GRACE AND RIGHTEOUSNESS

What gives us access to the presence of God?

Conviction has always been an indicator of the presence of God coming to His people. When His light shines into us, it exposes things we need to deal with and the godly sorrow we feel leads us to ask for and receive His forgiveness. But while repentance plays a vital part, revival won't sustain by repentance alone. If we believe that revival is fueled by repentance from sin, then we've got to find more sin to repent from; otherwise, we cannot sustain a move of God. But if we believe that revival comes from His presence then revival can be sustained indefinitely. The awakening we see beginning to birth across the globe is a presence-driven move of God.

If revival comes from hosting His presence, then we must ask, *What gives us access to His presence?* God's requirement is righteousness; so to live aware of His presence we need a revelation of His righteousness. We need to learn to live in the good of what He's done and understand that His sacrifice empowers us to abide in His presence. Now, if we're living in sin, deal with it, repent, and stop it. We can't learn to host the presence of God if we are tolerating sin in our life; however, despite our weaknesses, times of refreshing come from the presence of the Lord. We believe the revelation of His righteousness will transform our environment. We will be refreshed in His presence so that the power of His Spirit working in and through us can change the atmosphere and alter the way we view the world around us.

Called to Righteousness

The call of God on our lives includes an invitation to live fully righteous. God assured His covenant people that they were called in righteousness (Isa 42:6). He connects the fulfillment of His purpose for our lives to our understanding of how we appropriate His righteousness. To facilitate this, the Spirit of Grace points us to Jesus, the source of our righteousness, so we can pattern our lives after Him.

We find, unfortunately, a considerable amount of misunderstanding in the body of Christ about how righteousness works. Most believers know that we have received an imputed righteousness, given by God, which allows us to live in His presence. But, there is considerable disagreement about what that looks like and how deep that righteousness goes in us.

One of the marks of the current move of God is the

realization that we need to have more faith in God's righteousness than we have in our ability to keep His righteousness. We absolutely believe that repentance remains a key to revival, but we understand that as believers, <u>repentance doesn't come from a sin-conscious position; it comes from a righteous-conscious position.</u> In Christ, we should no longer see ourselves as sinners but as adopted sons and daughters of the King. When we repent and deal with things we've done wrong, we do it with a desire to remain in His favor and not with a view of gaining His favor. Once we have received His salvation we are immediately accepted by God because of what Jesus has done. His blood washed us clean and changed our identity. To participate in all God is doing we need to understand that righteousness comes as a gift received by faith in His amazing grace.

Righteousness by Faith

Paul told the Philippians that his goal was to ...*be found in Him, not having a righteousness of my own derived from the law, but that which is through faith in Christ, the righteousness which comes from God on the basis of faith* (Phil 3:9). The righteousness we need comes from God. It does not originate from our ability to do what God said; it comes from God as a gift through His abundant grace (Rom 5:17). When we received Christ as Savior, the Father declared us righteous through the blood of His Son. We can stand before Him complete and accepted by the virtue of what Jesus has done. We don't need a further work of righteousness, considering that we have received the perfect righteousness we need by faith.

We still need His grace to work in us to bring us into full sanctification, but God did the act of regeneration. That happened in us in coming to Christ, because only God can make us righteous enough to please Him. Now that's really good news, for it means that we don't have as much to do with this process as we thought. The moment we accepted Christ, God saw us in and through the righteousness of His Son. What an incredible truth!

Some appear to teach the grace of God with little accountability for personal holiness. We are concerned that the misunderstanding or misapplication of this truth about righteousness could prove a threat to the current move of God. If we teach a righteousness in which we have no responsibility, then we will end up with a sin problem, because those who are declared righteous still need to live in the good of the righteousness we have been given. But we don't live righteous in order to be accepted; we live righteous because we've been declared righteous and have a new nature at work in us. There's a huge difference between these two.

We're looking for a revival that has holiness at its core. Which means repentance will remain pivotal to accessing all God has done. However, the key to living in holiness comes when we choose to live in our new identity with a fresh appreciation for the righteousness that has been given to us by faith. In the context of stating that righteousness comes by faith (Rom 3:22), Paul reminds us that we have all sinned (Rom 3:23), and then immediately speaks of Jesus, displayed publicly as a sacrifice of atonement for our sin (Rom 3:25). This sequence is critical; we have received grace through this redemption paid by His blood, and in it, we find the faith to access His righteousness. The propitiation was a demonstration of His righteousness, and when we accept Him, we get to step into the good of what Jesus has done.

Grace at the Mercy Seat

The Greek word, *hilastérion*, is translated as "propitiation" (or sacrifice of atonement) in Romans, and "mercy seat" in the book of Hebrews (Rom 3:25, Heb 9:5). So our redemption takes place at the mercy seat, sometimes called the seat of grace. To better understand this connection, remember that on Mt Sinai, God instructed Moses to build the Ark of the Covenant that would represent the presence or dwelling place of God on the earth. It would be housed in the Holy of Holies, located in the inner court of the tabernacle, behind a curtain. This holy place full of His presence had only limited access.

Once a year, the high priests who had fulfilled the sacrifices and performed all the cleansing rituals had the privilege of stepping through the curtain into the Holy of Holies. Their one task there in the presence of God was to sprinkle the blood of the sacrifice on the mercy seat. No one else could ever witness the transaction, because from the moment Adam sinned, the daily fellowship they had enjoyed with God ceased. Sin created a barrier in their relationship and in their ability to communicate with their heavenly Father. The only way to restore the relationship with God was through sacrifice. With all the prescribed sacrifices done perfectly, God granted limited access to His presence.

With that understanding, look at the statement God included in His instructions for building the ark and mercy seat. Once he finished the process of construction, God told Moses, ...*there I will meet with you; and from above the mercy seat, from between the two cherubim which are upon the ark of the testimony* (Ex 25:22). What an amazing promise! This is the first time since the Garden of Eden that God promises to meet with man face-to-face. God guaranteed Moses that this life-changing encounter would happen at the mercy seat. The blood proved sufficient to cover sin, meaning that Moses could meet and come into a more intimate relationship with God. The perfect blood of the sacrifice granted access to Him, but it brought more than just access for a brief encounter.

The word *meet* used here is the same word used for *agreement* by prophet Amos when he wrote, *can two walk together, unless they be agreed?* (Amos 3:3 KJV). So the meeting God spoke of also carries the idea of a negotiated agreement. God told Moses that when the blood touched the Mercy seat God and man could come back into accord. This place of mercy gives us access and allows us to come into full reconciliation with our Father.

When Christ died, His blood was sprinkled on the mercy seat. Today, when we meet God at the mercy seat, He sees us as new creations. With the blood on the mercy seat, God looks across it into our face and sees us through the transforming power of the blood of His Son. When He looks at us, He doesn't see our past, our history, our failures, our mistakes, or even disappointments. He looks at us and sees us as the perfect righteousness of His Son; what a critical truth for us.

Eyes of Grace

The awakening growing across the earth requires the body of Christ to learn to live in a culture of honor with one another. A key for walking in honor is choosing to look at one another across the mercy seat in the same way that God looks at us. We don't look at others based on how they messed up (as easy as that is to do). We look at people based on how God sees them, righteous through the blood of His Son. The blood on the mercy seat changes everything. It allows us to see one another through eyes of grace.

For most of us as believers, this has been an area of great challenge and the source of some of our greatest failures. Most of us relate to the people around us based on what we see in the natural, instead of seeing them through the lens of grace, which equips us to recognize who they are in Christ. What if every time we looked at somebody, we saw him or her through the lens of the righteousness of Christ? It would change the way we view people. It would allow us to begin to call out their destiny, because we would see them as God sees them, rather than through the tainted filter of this natural realm. What if every member of the body of Christ began to look at people through that grid?

There is a covering involved in the agreement we find at the mercy seat. The mercy seat covered the ark, which housed the tablets of the law. If the mercy seat were removed, God would look at us across the tablets of the law. How many of the Ten Commandments have we broken this week? That's His view without the mercy seat. How depressing! Without the blood, God looks at us on the basis of what we have done, the filthy rags of our own righteousness. So we walk with our head down, afraid to even look up, fearing His condemnation and judgment. But with the mercy seat in place, the blood of the Son allows God to see us fully redeemed.

He sees us through the righteousness that His Son achieved and not through our failure to keep the law. Why is this so important? Because revival is sustained by the presence of God and if we hesitate to come into His presence because of something we have done, we will never see the move of God that we believe for. But if we have free access to His presence through the righteousness of the Son, then we can come in and enjoy Him as men and women who have been forgiven, cleansed, and sustained by His grace.

This could get powerful. If our belief would change, it would alter the way we think. So let's make sure we understand exactly what happened. Jesus said, *I did not come to abolish the law, but to fulfill it* (Matt 5:17). Jesus didn't come to take the Ten Commandments out of the ark. He came to completely fulfill God's law so that the blood He shed would be fully righteous; only righteous blood can impart righteousness to us. The blood of the sacrifice in Moses' tabernacle would only temporarily make it possible for the priest to come into the presence of God. But the righteous blood of the Son sprinkled on the mercy seat gives us permanent access into the Holy of Holies. To emphasize this truth, at the moment of Christ's death the Father tore the veil that had barred access to the Holy of Holies. This symbol of the separation, which had existed since Adam, was torn in two from top to bottom by the hands of God.

Perfect Righteousness

We find this gift of righteousness Jesus made available to us through His grace more wonderful than we have imagined. His righteousness is not given to us based on our history; it is applied to us based on Jesus' history. Look at what He said at His baptism. John did not want to baptize Jesus, but He answered, *It is fitting for us to fulfill all righteousness* (Matt 3:15). He understood the responsibility to fulfill all righteousness in order to become the perfect unblemished sacrifice. From the time He turned twelve, His parents had taken Him to the temple, fulfilling every requirement of the law. He knew that this baptism of repentance was necessary to fulfill all righteousness. He fulfilled every detailed specification so that when He shed His blood, it would be perfectly righteous, creating a righteousness that He can now gift to us.

When He came up out of the water, heaven opened, and a voice from heaven confirmed His identity. *This is my beloved Son in whom I am well pleased* (Matt 3:17). The Holy Spirit descended on Him and for the first time in human history, the Holy Spirit came to remain on the earth. Why? Because Jesus was fully righteous and righteousness opens heaven. When we are righteous, we have access to the Father's affirmation. When we are righteous we live under an open heaven, because we know we are restored to His family and we stand acceptable to Him.

The perfect, complete righteousness that Jesus lived was poured out on the mercy seat at His death. When God looks at us across the mercy seat, He sees in us a heaven-opening righteousness. He sees those who have received the sacrifice of the Son as fully righteous and He willingly gives us the Holy Spirit. Let's begin to live out our calling with a revelation of the mercy seat. The call of God is an invitation to sit across from Him at the mercy seat, with our identity fully in His righteousness. Remember during the Brownsville Revival, one of the invitation songs focused on running to the Mercy Seat; what a great song for revival. Now that we understand that refreshing comes from His presence, the mercy seat takes on fresh significance as the place where the truth of our new identity becomes a reality.

Reversing the Lie

The enemy comes to steal, kill and destroy (John 10:10). He speaks condemnation and reminds us constantly of our failures and inadequacies. But one thing we know, everything the enemy says is either a lie or distortion of the truth. So, if he only speaks lies, then the opposite must be the truth. If we start hearing it correctly, his words can stir faith. When we live with a revelation of the mercy seat, we know that if the enemy says we can't, it means we can. If he says we are not qualified, then we must be qualified. If he's saying we don't know enough, then we must know enough. If he's saying we haven't studied enough, then we probably have. If he's saying we haven't prayed enough (of course we need to pray); but we pray from victory, not from defeat, and with a revelation of righteousness, we pray under an open heaven.

When we understand His righteousness, it changes the way we view the world and the people around us. What if when we looked at other believers, we saw them as heaven sees them, through the righteousness of Christ? The church might actually start becoming the kingdom people that Jesus envisioned. We might start responding to people from what Christ has done and not based on what they've done. What a novel idea! We need to have more confidence in His ability to bring us into full sanctification than we have in our own ability to get there. We should have tremendous confidence that He who began the work can complete His good work in us. With a revelation of the mercy seat, we should have absolute confidence that He will bring us to maturity.

Self-Righteousness

We won't reach maturity unless we understand that righteousness doesn't come because of anything we've done; it comes because of what Jesus did. One of the greatest threats to the call of God on our lives comes from the problem of self-righteousness. While telling a series of parables to the Pharisees after He had cleansed the temple, Jesus makes the statement that ...*many are called but few are chosen* (Matt 22:14). The invitation goes out to all but only a few choose to respond. This is not specifically a reference to the church, implying that only a few of those He called would be chosen, but rather a statement that the call had gone out to His people but few were responding to him. The context was a parable about a guest invited to a feast who showed up wearing the wrong garment. One had chosen to clothe himself in his own garment instead of accepting the one the master had offered. The Master's garment we must accept and wear is the righteousness of the Son.

Self-righteousness poses a big issue. We find it so easy to try to do enough to feel acceptable to God. Paul warns the church in Rome about this when he wrote, ... *not knowing about God's righteousness and seeking to establish their own, they*

SECTION ONE

did not subject themselves to the righteousness of God (Rom 10:3). He cautioned them that they needed to subject themselves to the righteousness of God. "Subject" is a great word; it means to submit under or to put ourselves at the mercy of the righteousness of God. The people Paul referred to had not grasped the fact that God had already gifted righteousness to them, so they tried to establish a righteousness on their own. It probably felt right to them, but such self-righteousness works against us, causing us to slip into shame or judging others.

If we don't understand the power of His righteousness, we can't live the transformed lives He called us to. We will live "sin conscious," focused on our failures and not recognizing our identity as new creations. This leads to countless futile attempts to clean up our lives, which only result in the filthy rags of self-righteousness. We need to live in the good of the gift of righteousness He has given us and shake off the stuff that keeps hanging on. We can't fulfill our call living only on the repentance side of the cross; we must live secure in the righteousness purchased for us on the cross. The blood of Christ on the mercy seat provides much more than a temporary covering based on what we've done. It releases a permanent righteousness based on what Jesus did, so we can subject ourselves to His righteousness and let go of our own.

When we put our trust in His righteousness, we can trust God to finish the work He started in us. We finally understand that no amount of effort on our part can ever produce a righteousness good enough to please Him. Jesus said it this way, ...*unless your righteousness surpasses that of the Scribes and Pharisees, you shall not enter the Kingdom of Heaven* (Matt 5:20). Wow, the Scribes and Pharisees were as righteous as anyone in their day. They lived in detailed adherence to the law, yet with all the self-sacrifice and all the discipline, it still wasn't enough to make them acceptable to God.

A Higher Standard

Then Jesus raised the bar even higher with the Sermon on the Mount. Where the law says don't murder, He said, don't even get angry with our neighbor. When the law says don't commit adultery, He said, don't even look at a woman with lust in your heart. Jesus raised righteousness to a level impossible for us to reach, but He lived it. He lived in perfect obedience to the law. So we have to decide, are we going to trust our ability to get it right; will we trust our ability to say the right things, to do the right things, to express the right things? Or will we trust ourselves to the righteousness of God? Which will prove more trustworthy? We would rather trust His ability to impart and impute to us His righteousness as a gift than to trust our ability to get it right.

When we live consciously aware of His gift of righteousness it changes us. Every morning we wake up seeing ourselves seated at the mercy seat, knowing that through the blood of Christ, God now views us through the reflection of what Jesus has done. It will change the way we live, it will change the way we treat others, and it will change the way we minister. Faith in His righteousness will keep us from the trap of self-righteousness. *For what does scripture say? Abraham believed God and it was reckoned to him as righteousness* (Rom 4:3). Even before Christ's blood on the mercy seat, Abraham put his faith in God and that act of faith was counted to him as righteousness. If this was true for Abraham, it can certainly be true for us. The more we trust Him, the more of His righteousness we appropriate. Isn't that what this verse says? Do we dare believe it? Can we trust that God really is that good?

Paul repeats this theme of righteousness by faith several times in his writings. He tells us that, *the Gentiles who did not pursue righteousness attained righteousness, even the righteousness which is by faith.* Read this carefully. The Gentiles who did not pursue righteousness attained righteousness by faith. *But Israel pursuing a law of righteousness did not arrive at that law. Why? Because they did not pursue it by faith, but as though it were by works. They stumbled over the stumbling stone* (Rom 9:30-32). How easy we find it to stumble over this idea of righteousness coming to us only by faith. We too often trip over the stumbling stone by reverting to a works-oriented mentality where we try to make ourselves acceptable to God rather than trusting His grace.

Many of us spend our entire life trying to get what we already have. We try to make ourselves acceptable to God, not realizing that we already are because of what Jesus had done. What if as believers we stop trying to get there and we lived as if we were there? What if as believers we began to believe that the righteousness of Christ given to us as a gift is sufficient to restore our fellowship with the Father? What if we began to live from a place of acceptance, not from a place of trying to gain approval? When we live from intimacy, sin doesn't become as big an issue because we want to please Him more than we want to sin. We enjoy the fellowship we have with our Father so much that we just don't have any desire to mess it up. We have the righteousness of Christ that comes to us when we put our faith in His amazing grace. Pray this with us:

Father forgive us for our tendency to trust our own righteousness instead of fully depending on the incredible gift You have offered. From this moment we place our trust in the righteousness of Christ and lay down all our attempts at self-righteousness. We choose to daily remind ourselves that it is the gift of righteousness that secures our identity. Holy Spirit, we ask you to convict us each time we drift away from grace and back into our own worthless self-effort. It is our desire to live confidently as Your sons and daughters, fully trusting Your abundant grace and gift of righteousness.

2

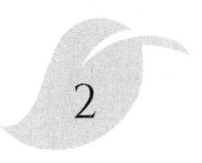

GRACE AND IDENTITY

What place does sin have in our new identity?

We have looked in depth at the gift of righteousness and recognized that when we put our faith in the grace of God and receive His gift of righteousness a profound exchange takes place in our identity. In this section, we will explore the nature of this new identity. In the book of Romans Paul gives us an exciting in-depth look at the work Jesus did and the transforming power of the new nature we receive when we accept His gift of salvation.

Remember the Romans did not know the law; that was not their background or their history. They approached their salvation from a different perspective. They received salvation through an incredible grace-filled message that brought them into the family of God. And although they had joyfully received the message, it is clear from their question that they didn't yet understand the power of their new identity to free them from sin.

We see this when Paul writes, *what shall we say then? Are we to continue in sin that grace might increase?* (Rom 6:1). What an odd thing to say. Paul didn't just think up this statement. He's obviously responding either to a question, or to a discussion that had taken place, perhaps even a letter that had been sent to him. Somewhere in the minds of the Gentile Church, the way they had processed grace led them to the question - does grace mean we should sin more so we get more grace? It's a legitimate question, but it comes out of not yet understanding the nature or power of grace. It comes from not realizing that God who loved us so much, has given us an incredible gift, and that our response to His gift is to align ourselves with Him so that sin is no longer normal or common for us.

When we come to Him and receive His incredible gift of grace, the outworking of that grace moves us away from sin, instead of towards sin. We so enjoy this release of grace that it draws us into a place where we no longer want to participate in the things that used to entice us. We no longer want to engage in the things that used to attract us because we've become recipients of something precious. We've found a once-hidden treasure and we're willing to give up everything else for the love of this one thing. We want to live as a friend of God, empowered by His grace enabling us to live free from sin.

Paul goes on in the next verse to respond to their question with an emphatic, *may it never be!* (Rom 6:2) He states in no uncertain terms that their question exposed a distortion of the truth. The question implied that they understood their sins were forgiven, but that the grace they received had them wondering about the source. They want more but don't yet understand that as a recipient of grace they're transformed. They don't realize the recreation that took place in their inner man giving them a new nature. They don't understand that the power of sin no longer has a legal hold over them; they are free.

A New Nature

Breaking free from the bondage to sin stands at the heart of the transforming power of grace. In the act of receiving His great salvation, we also received a new nature that is not under the control of our old sin nature. When we grasp this, grace starts having a greater impact on our lives. His transforming grace works to change our identity. The liberty from sin provides the confidence to fulfill our calling. That change will cause us not just to receive His grace and forgiveness but will actually empower us to live victoriously. Okay, we know this happened theologically but how do we begin practically to live in this reality?

Paul follows up his exclamation with a question. *How shall we who died to sin still live in it?* (Rom 6:2). He goes on to say that if we really understand this message of grace, we will understand that the old nature in us has literally died in the process of redemption. It no longer exists. Sin should not have power over us any longer. Through the grace of God, we died to the old nature we inherited from Adam. We must then treat sin as something that no longer has control over us. The root of the question about continuing to sin implies that the person knew they were forgiven for their sins but did not yet know that they had a new nature.

Paul goes on later in the chapter to give us the mindset we need in order to live in the reality of this truth. He makes the statement, *even so consider yourselves to be dead to sin, but alive to God in Christ Jesus* (Rom 6:11). He instructs us that the way we process this message of grace is to think of ourselves as dead to sin. When we contemplate our new identity, meditate on the fact that our old nature died. Because it is dead it has lost its power over us. How many of us woke up this morning and thought, whew, I'm dead to sin? We suspect not many. But Paul says that's how we live in grace. That's how change happens in our life.

Think Feel Act

Being an engineer I like formulas and one of my favorites involves the relationship between thinking, feeling, and acting. How we think will have an effect on how we feel, which in turn has a direct impact on how we act. Merely adjusting our behavior does not change our actions long-term. If it did, prison would work well. Sure, actions were adjusted but often people come out of incarceration with the same old thinking patterns . . . nothing's really changed. They simply served their time but there's no lasting effect. Change happens when our thinking changes. The change in our thinking begins to adjust how we feel and that causes our actions to follow as they line up with our revised beliefs.

We must learn to think differently about the power of sin if we want to live free from its attraction. Many of us struggle with habits, attitudes and behaviors that damage us and affect our relationships with others. To break out of these destructive cycles, we must learn to think differently, which causes us to feel different, and as a consequence, we're going to act different. This begins by choosing to believe that we truly are dead to sin regardless of how we feel.

Breaking the Power of Habitual Sin

It starts with acknowledging that some of our habits are sin. Too often we treat these things lightly. But in our heart we know it's wrong, especially when we've felt the Holy Spirit's conviction and yet we've procrastinated. This applies to so many things. The act itself may not seem like a sin, but if we damage our body with our behavior, and the Spirit has warned us to stop, we're walking in disobedience.

Part of the reason grace doesn't work for us is that we haven't treated the sin as sin. We treat it as our weakness, so our failing becomes acceptable. We convince ourselves that our broken behavior doesn't equate to sin; we are just weak in that area and we even begin to treat deficiency like a friend. We make peace with our shortcomings, having decided that the defect is just part of our identity. It's not really sinning; it's just my weakness. But if we would deal with it as sin, then we can apply grace to our failure and we could actually come into freedom.

The apostle Paul speaks directly to this issue. *Therefore do not let sin reign in your mortal body that you should obey its lusts, and do not go on presenting the members of your body to sin as instruments of unrighteousness; but present yourselves to God as those alive from the dead, and your members as instruments of righteousness to God. For sin shall not be master over you, for you are not under law, but under grace* (Rom 6:12-14). To access the grace of God we must first acknowledge the things that have mastered us. Only then can we submit these weaknesses to the transforming power of grace.

This will cause us to look at the thing that has controlled us in a whole new light. When we understand how grace works, we realize that the road to freedom begins with learning to think differently about the things that have held us in bondage. We come to know that as long as we agree with the lie that our old nature is alive, we empower that lie to bring destruction into our life. But when we learn to think of ourselves as dead to sin, we will begin to feel and walk in sync with the grace of God.

Stinking Thinking

Paul gives a strong caution about the effect of wrong thinking when he writes, *this I say therefore, and affirm together with the Lord, that you walk no longer just as the Gentiles also walk, in the futility of their mind* (Eph 4:17). This is an admonition about the effect of wrong thinking. He warns them that their behavior had to do with old thinking patterns. We must deal with the way we think because, if we don't deal with our thought life, we won't find the fortitude to change our feelings or behaviors. We simply won't be able to overcome it.

He is speaking to the Gentiles, which includes anybody who wasn't born a Jew. It referred to all those who had no covenant and no future promise. Gentiles were seen as outside of the camp with no access to the purpose of God. But now, in Christ, God in His grace has grafted us into all of these promises. Paul challenges those who have come out of this history to change the way they think. He says, "I don't want you to think like a Gentile." He is referring to a thinking pattern in which we have no hope and no access to becoming part of the family of God. When we think like a Gentile we have no aspiration of ever getting free because we can't even imagine salvation. When we think that way we are going to feel that way and we will act out of that broken identity.

When we think like a sinner we will feel like a sinner and sin will still be normal for us. We sing hymns about being a sinner saved by grace. But when we sing it we tend to put more emphasis on the "I'm a sinner" than we do on the "saved by grace." Every time we do, we reinforce the lie that we're not really dead to sin.

Paul says that every day when we wake up, we need to die to what's behind us. Every morning we need to treat our old nature as dead because when we wake up, the stinking thinking wants to wake up with us. When we get up, it wants to get up with us and reinforce the old patterns of our life. We must, by choice, change our thinking so that when we wake, our first thought is alive with the glory of our new identity. We then will live secure in the freedom that grace brings. When Paul tells us to consider ourselves dead to sin he uses the word *logizomia*, which meant to gather up all the facts and make a decision based on the truth. Can it really be true that the old man is dead? Yes! Because of the power of grace, it is true; and if we will begin to treat the old man as dead, we will live in the blessing of this incredible deliverance.

Forming Callouses

Not only were the Gentiles trapped in stinking thinking, their broken identity also interfered with their ability to understand. Paul says they were *darkened in their understanding*. What happens when we think incorrectly? Our understanding gets fuzzy. We lose our ability to reason, so we fail to discern the truth. Our conscience justifies our behavior and no longer measures it against the standard of the Word of God. We no longer appreciate the truth, so we do what seems right to us.

What's the next thing the Word says? The result of this dysfunction is that we are *excluded from the life of God*. How many of us honestly have ever felt excluded from the life of God? If we have, we don't understand His grace. If we have accepted the salvation Jesus paid for and we still feel excluded, then our feelings are lying to us. Our feelings are still connected to a thinking pattern that ties us to our old sin nature, which will cause us to behave in a way that is inconsistent with the truth. Because I think like a sinner, I feel I'm a sinner, and I act like I'm nothing more than a poor, miserable sinner.

Now, do we still have the propensity to sin? You bet, every morning we wake up and there "it" is, that decaying, stinking thinking that we thought we put to death yesterday. It must be a daily discipline we exercise each morning. In fact, if you're like us, you might have to do it several times a day to keep your thinking right.

What's next? They were excluded *because of the ignorance that is in them, because of the hardness of their heart and they, having become callous* (Eph 4:18, 19). Because of the drift into sin their conscience has become calloused. What's a callous? That place that just gets rubbed so long it becomes hard and desensitized. When we give in to sin our hearts grow calloused, so that when we have participated in sinful behavior long enough, it feels normal.

The habit becomes our identity. We tolerate our sin and decide that people just need to accept us for who we are. A callous has rubbed onto our heart, so we no longer behave as a child of God that's been set free by the power of His grace. Because our thinking remains distorted and our understanding is cloudy, we behave like somebody that is still bound to an old nature. That's the Roman question, should we just sin more so we get more grace, No! *You did not learn Christ in this way* (Eph 4:20). Reckon the thing dead so that we can become a recipient of the changing power of God and begin to live out of our new nature; that's where grace will take us. We don't want grace just for forgiveness, we want grace for change, and we want grace for living life in the new nature that He purchased for us on the cross.

Nature Restored in Him

Adam and Eve in the garden enjoyed an incredible level of fellowship and daily intimacy with God. They were supplied with all the resources necessary to do the work they needed to do in the garden. They were created with a divine purpose, to rule over God's creation, and to subdue anything that would seek to disrupt the atmosphere. Adam and Eve were created with a perfect nature, a nature in complete harmony with God's character.

But in the fall they lost all these benefits. They lost the daily fellowship they enjoyed with their Creator. They were driven out of the Garden, losing access to the resources they had enjoyed, substituting abundance for sweat and toil. They lost their purpose; having abdicated their authority, they no longer implemented the rule of heaven on earth. Finally, in a devastating exchange, they traded in their perfect nature for a sin nature that no longer reflected God's character.

But now in Christ, we see a full restoration of all that was lost in the fall. In Christ our access to the Father is restored so that we can again have daily fellowship. In Christ we are granted access to the resources of heaven; our adoption into the family of God guarantees that our loving Father gladly takes care of His kids. In Christ we have a restored purpose and can once again participate in the advancement of the Kingdom of God here on earth. Finally, in Christ we have a new nature. Our old man is dead, buried with Him in baptism and we have been raised up as new creations in Christ through the power of His resurrected life.

To the Colossians, *Paul says for in Him all the fulness of Deity dwells in bodily form, and in Him you have been made complete and in Him you were also circumcised with a circumcision made without hands, in the removal of the body of the flesh by the circumcision of Christ* (Col 2:9-11). Just to be clear, does this suggest the temporary removal of the body of flesh? No, that's not what it says; it promises that in Christ the old nature is removed! What happens when you remove something? It is gone, cut off, disposed of. The sin nature has been cut out through identification with Jesus' death and we live in this reality through a powerful work of the Holy

Spirit. We've got to change our thinking because, generally, we don't think of our sin nature as removed.

Dead and Buried

Now the enemy tries to convince us that our old nature is alive and well, but it's a lifeless, powerless lie. Our legal standing before God is that our sin nature was removed in a divine circumcision. Circumcision is the cutting off of something that is extraneous. The impediment gets cut out of the way so it can't interfere with our life in Christ. Read it again, *having been buried with Him in baptism, in which you were also raised up with Him through faith in the working of God* (Col 2:12). Don't you want to get baptized again? This Scripture indicates that we should view baptism as more than a symbolic act; it is a profound identification with His death and a participation in His resurrection life.

Any ordinance like baptism, we do by faith and we receive by faith. So what should we believe for in baptism; what should we expect? If we believe baptism is only a symbolic public confession, when we go down into the water, we get wet but very little of significance happens. But if we receive baptism by faith, then it becomes a testimony and a declaration that something got cut out and left behind in the grave. We can affirm that the sin nature no longer has control; the legal tie to that way of thinking and living is broken. We need to think differently, and if we think differently, we will feel differently, and if we feel differently, we'll act differently.

SECTION TWO

Too many of us still try to adjust our actions by disciplining our outward behavior instead of going to the root and changing our thinking. One method seeks to find maturity from the outside in, while the other works so that we are changed from the inside out. But in fact, only when transformed thinking affects our actions, will our actions be permanently changed. We need some things permanently changed. We need to come to a place that we reckon our old nature dead so that it doesn't have control over us anymore.

Go back to the beginning of Romans six and look at a few more verses. *Or do you not know that all of us who have been baptized into Christ Jesus have been baptized into His death? Therefore we have been buried with Him through baptism into death, in order that as Christ was raised from the dead through the glory of the Father, so we too might walk in newness of life* (Rom 6:3-4). In baptism, we identified with His death in a profound way. We participated in His death. When He died, I died. His death has become my death. And what did we die to? We died to our history, we died to our failures, we died to generational bondages; but even more profoundly, we died to sin. We left our old nature behind when we came up out of that water. In an act of divine mercy, the old nature that we inherited from Adam was circumcised out of us and it has been replaced by a new nature.

Look at the next verse, *knowing this, that our old self was crucified with Him, that our body of sin might be done away with, that we should no longer be slaves to sin; for he who has died is freed from sin* (Rom 6:6, 7). The old man was crucified with Him and the body of sin done away with. What an incredible thought! Because of this divine exchange, we no longer serve as slaves to sin. The moment we die in Him the old nature dies with us, freeing us from the curse of the fall.

Alive in Christ

But it is not just a death, it is also a resurrection; go back a couple of verses, *for if we have become united with Him in the likeness of His death, certainly we shall be also in the likeness of His resurrection* (Rom 6:5). By faith we also identify with His resurrection. If we abide in Him, then Christ's resurrection from the dead becomes our resurrection. Scripture tells us that in Christ we are a new creation; the old is gone, left behind in the grave (2 Cor. 5:17). But it doesn't stop there. We came up out of the grave with Him and everything has been made new. Through identification with His resurrection, we can live as a new creation made in the image of our creator.

It is time to live in the good of this magnificent gift and to ask ourselves some serious questions. Do we believe this truth or do we find it more familiar to fight daily against the phantom power of sin? What should our identification with His death and resurrection accomplish in us? What is God's end goal for the new nature? What should this awesome grace produce in us? We must come into alignment with His truth about our new nature if we ever hope to step into all He has planned for us. Stop for a moment and pray this with us:

Father, help us to understand Your grace to change. Help us to understand that what has happened in us needs to produce a profound breaking of our old thought patterns. Bring us to a place of revelation and understanding of who You are and what You have done. Lord, right now, we want to understand the grace to change. We don't want to be the same next year. We don't want to stay in the same place. We don't want to struggle with the same issues. We want the grace to change, Lord. We position ourselves to allow Your Spirit to challenge some of the things we've believed. Lord, give us the grace to get really hungry, desperate for Your life to be poured out into us. Father, right now we surrender to You and ask You to touch us by the power of Your Spirit.

GRACE EMPOWERED HOLINESS

Is it possible to meet God's standard of holiness?

Holiness is the foundational aspect of God's nature; it characterizes the integrity of His own being. The "Holy, holy, holy" that both Isaiah and John heard resounding in the throne room establishes God's complete and absolute holiness. In a Semitic language words are repeated for emphasis. Holiness is the only attribute of God where we find this three-fold intensity making it a foundation of His nature. This attention given to His holiness, means God never needs to choose to be good, loving, or gracious. He doesn't strive to accomplish what we would define as "being holy." Instead, because God's very essence is holy, He can never behave in less than a holy manner. God is holy in every attribute, every thought and in every action.

Having described God's absolute holiness, the Bible

then calls us to be holy. This raises the question, where does holiness come from? We believe there has often been a misunderstanding about this, which causes us to try to produce holiness from self-effort. When this happens, believers get into an endless cycle of failure and remorse that stunts their growth toward spiritual maturity. Instead, God does something supernatural to release holiness into us. To appropriate this, we need a fresh revelation of the sanctifying work of the Holy Spirit in our lives.

God requires holiness from us: affirmed by the command to *be holy, for I am holy* (1 Pet 1:16). We know this verse well and in fact, we find some form of this statement repeated several times in scripture. So it's not an injunction that we can ignore. It is sobering to realize the magnitude of God's assumption that we can walk in holiness. God expects us in some way to mirror His own holiness. While this may not refer to His absolute holiness, it certainly describes a relational holiness we can and must emulate. The challenge we have is that when we look at the command, we read it through the lens of disciplining ourselves to put in the effort to live up to His standard. The very thought that success is based on our own ability to be perfectly self-disciplined makes it feel out of reach.

But to answer the dilemma, look at the same verse in another translation that picks up a truth not always clear. Some translate the verse as, *you must be holy because I am holy* (1 Pet 1:16 NIV, NLT). Notice, it does not read be holy

<u>like</u> I am holy, but be holy <u>because</u> I am holy. The causative "because" makes a huge difference. In fact, at least eight versions translate this verse with the causative. The holiness in Him has the power to <u>cause</u> us to be holy. A causative means that the subject causes the action in the object. Something happens because someone else initiated it. With a causative, the effect on us takes place because the Subject, God, did something. That's really important because He does not ask us to be holy without His help; we're asked to be holy by the power of the Spirit at work in us that causes us to be holy.

The alternate wordings for this verse conjure up different images in our mind. When we think about the first one, "be <u>holy</u> like I am holy," the picture forms in our mind of a boss shaking his finger in our face saying, "You've got to be holy. Do it like I do it!" And we walk away from the encounter feeling ashamed and powerless, thinking we must do better, we must try harder and we must find more discipline. Somehow we feel we have to change what we're doing so that we can conform to the way He expects us to perform.

But the causative, "be holy <u>because</u> I am holy," conjures up a very different scenario. If we search the internet for an image of "causative," almost all of the results show pictures of germs. The bacteria and viruses represent the things that cause illness. So instead of the idea of the boss shaking his finger in our face, in a causative image we get the idea of our boss sneezing on us, and the flu germ in him got into us, giving us the flu. This seems a somewhat irreverent picture, but it is an accurate representation of a causative at work. God breathed on us and the contagious nature of His holiness got into us, causing us to become holy. That's a causative. God's holiness has regenerative power that does something in us so that, from the inside out, we begin producing holiness. Not by trying to conform to something, but because something inside us changed; we've caught something. We have caught the creative nature of His holiness.

To be Like Jesus

Look at the previous verse, *but like the Holy One who called you, be holy ... in all your behavior* (1 Pet 1:15). At first glance, this sounds like a simple instruction to imitate God's behavior, but let's take a closer look at the words. First, the word "like" here is a preposition that means "according to or down from." Then, the verb "to be" used here is a causative form of become. If we look in the margins of our Bible, we'll find both, "according to" and "become," referenced as alternate translations for these words. Now look at how the verse reads with these definitions substituted in. *But according to what's flowing down from the Holy One who called you to become holy;* holiness is being formed in us as it flows down to us from His nature. He is the model of holiness. We live out His holiness because it is flowing down to us from Him by His Spirit, causing us to be holy in all our behavior. We need to start operating out of the revelation of what His grace has caused to happen in us through what He did on the cross.

SECTION THREE

When we operate securely in our grace-based identity, the connection with our Creator causes us to grow to reflect His holiness. We need to shift our expectation of where holiness comes from. Paul wrote, *therefore, having these promises, beloved, let us cleanse ourselves from all filthiness of the flesh and spirit, perfecting holiness in the fear of God* (2 Cor. 7:1). Again, it's easy to read a verse like this and immediately hear self-effort. Now, we're not saying we don't need to obey the word. Please don't hear that, but if we're trying to be holy by putting on external forms, we will get in trouble. Where does holiness come from? The context of this verse is the amazing promise that as adopted sons and daughters, we're connected to God in a living, unique way. The spiritual DNA in us has changed.

In the divine exchange of salvation, we were born again into a family. It wasn't just a legal adoption; it was a new birth into a real family so that we now live under the influence of the life that flows out of that family. God sneezed on us. Something amazing happened and a bug of holiness infected us. Hallelujah! His holiness starts working on the inside of us, changing the nature of the way we think, the way we talk, and the way we act. Paul understood the gospel of grace as well as anyone, yet he extorts us to pursue a lifestyle of holiness and to walk in the fear of the Lord. He calls on us to live separate from sin, perfecting holiness – but how do we do this? Do we work on this to produce it or are we missing something?

To Timothy Paul writes, *God, who has saved us, and called us with a holy calling, not according to our works, but according to His own purpose and grace which was granted us in Christ Jesus from all eternity* (2 Tim 1:9-10). First, we see that our calling is a holy calling, making holiness a vital part of our new identity. We're connected to a holy calling, which makes holiness the way we live our lives. There's holiness in the call. But the second part of that verse is that we're called according to His purpose and His grace. So our calling is connected directly to how well we understand our purpose and how much we receive His grace. If we are not receiving His grace correctly, we're not going to fulfill our calling correctly. We might go through a form of our calling; but without the grace, we'll never produce lasting fruit. There's a grace component of holiness that God wants to put into us. Our calling will only function correctly when it's tied to His purpose and powered by His grace. But to live in the benefits of grace we must avoid any mindset that nullifies the power of grace.

The Trap of Legalism

The first enemy of grace takes the form of pursuing holiness through legalistic self-effort. When Paul wrote the Galatians to deal with their legalism, he challenged their understanding of the source of their sanctification. The Galatians were slipping back into a mindset of legalism, and his caution to them was, *having begun in the Spirit, are you now being made perfect by the flesh?* (Gal 3:3). Having been birthed into our new identity by the Holy Spirit, can we now come into the perfection God has for us by our own self-effort? Paul contends that we must not abandon the grace that brought us here. The grace that brought us this far is the grace that's going to keep us here, and the grace that's going to sanctify us.

Christian life is lived by grace. We are saved by grace, and we are sanctified or made holy by the same grace. His grace causes us to be holy. Walking in holiness is essential; but if we approach it based on self-effort or outward conformity to rules and regulations, we strive and live under bondage. *Pursuing holiness through legalistic self-effort circumvents the work of Jesus and nullifies the grace of God.* Self-effort destroys the power of the sneeze. It literally inoculates us against the sanctifying work of the Holy Spirit. Self-effort says we don't really need that; what we need is to try really, really hard and then we can do it. But God says that He wants to do something in us that produces holiness because the seed of holiness has been planted inside us. Something was released into us that has the power to free us from self-effort so that we can be changed by the power of His grace. Can we trust grace? Can we trust that His grace has that much power?

The Snare of License

The second enemy that nullifies grace is the belief that grace somehow removes the requirement for holiness.

While we can't pursue holiness out of legalistic self-effort, grace does not remove the requirement to live holy - grace *does not* change God's standard. There are popular teachers in the body of Christ today who concern us because they appear to teach a grace that no longer requires that we walk in holiness. Grace doesn't remove the mandate of holiness; instead, His grace empowers us to fulfill it. Peter speaks of the sanctifying work of the Spirit (1 Pet 1:2). The word sanctify is a compound word combining *sanctus* meaning holy and *facio* meaning to make. So the work of the Holy Spirit is to make us holy. The Holy Spirit who birthed us into Jesus, works in us, making us holy. Holiness is never removed from the equation, because it's a crucial part of being formed into Christ's image.

If for whatever reason we tolerate an area of unholiness in our life, we must deal with it. We need to invite the Holy Spirit to come and deposit new life in us. The Spirit of Holiness in us will manifest holiness in our nature if we'll give Him permission. The holiness virus we have been infected by will produce something in us, changing the way we behave. This change in behavior comes from that internal work of the Holy Spirit. *Any teaching of grace that removes God's requirement of holiness is an affront to His sacrifice.* It is a violation. The Father sacrificed His Son so that we could come back into a right relationship and be holy. The holiness that was lost in the fall is restored in Christ. Don't get duped into believing that grace somehow provides the liberty to sin. That's the challenge the Romans had when they asked Paul their question about sin and grace.

The woman caught in adultery gives a perfect picture of the connection between grace and holiness. This woman was caught in adultery and they dragged her out to be stoned. Some of the teachers of the law decided to use it as a test case to accuse Jesus, so they brought her to Him to make their public accusation. The teachers of the law had the legal right to stone her for what she had done. But Jesus did this incredible thing; He stooped down and wrote something on the ground. (When we get to heaven, I want to check out the YouTube video of this encounter to find out what He wrote). Whatever He wrote, all the accusers left. Jesus manifested the grace of God to her in a most profound way, but then immediately said, *go and sin no more* (Jn. 8:11).

The grace He released to the woman had the power to allow her to walk away and sin no more. Get this down inside us. The grace He released had the power to cause her to forsake sin and live free from her history. The grace she received did not remove the requirement to be holy, but unlike the law, it actually empowered her to walk in holiness. The grace on Him got into her and infected her with the germ of holiness. Jesus sneezed on her! We must come to trust the grace of God to do the work of sanctification in us.

Instructed by Grace

Grace is our instructor in the journey into holiness.

Look at what Paul told Titus. *For the grace of God that brings salvation has appeared to all men, teaching us that, denying ungodliness and worldly lusts, we should live soberly, righteously, and godly in the present age, looking for the blessed hope and glorious appearing of our great God and Savior Jesus Christ* (Titus 2:11-13). It says: "grace teaches us." If we will trust His grace, it will teach us to be holy. The sneeze deposited a virus, a seed of holiness that the Holy Spirit brings to life in us so that we begin to manifest the life that flows down from His nature. We are infected with holiness because His nature has been put into us.

The grace of God awakens our conscience with a desire for holiness. We will learn to walk in holiness, not because we try harder, but because we submit to the teacher. We must yield to the internal work of the Holy Spirit, trusting Him to produce something that we can't produce ourselves. We need to trust the grace of God administered by the Spirit of God to do something in us to change our character and behavior. Grace works in us, not because we've tried really hard, but because we have placed our trust in its transforming power.

I grew up in a very legalistic home. We did have a relationship with God, but it was based on so many externals. Sunday was the worst day of my life because when we weren't in church, we had to sit in the living room with the Bible open in our lap, reading it. And when you're young and the sun is shining and the birds are singing, you want to be outside, playing. We really didn't want to be in the house, sitting with the Bible on our lap. Then when I went to college, I had an encounter with the Holy Spirit and something inside me changed. The effect started to transform my behavior. I began to live victoriously because I had been touched on the inside, not because I was trying harder.

Before the encounter I was a Christian; I gave my life to Jesus when I was 3 years old. My parents reminded me regularly about my conversion experience. I knew Jesus loved me. I knew He died for me, but I was trying really hard to live up to expectations. Then the sneeze happened. Something was deposited inside me by the power of the Spirit. In a moment, things that used to control me lost their power. They weren't hard to lay down. The *grace of God that brings salvation* teaches us to deny ungodliness and worldly lusts and to live *soberly, righteously, and godly*. The true grace of God doesn't simply remove the guilt of sin; instead, it actually empowers us to live holy from the inside out. Grace teaches us to be holy.

A word of caution: If the grace we received isn't teaching us to be holy, we need to reevaluate the grace we received. Grace alone has the ability to transform us into the image of Christ. Every one of us wants that on some level; we want to walk in His image. But do we succeed by putting on external controls or by yielding to the Holy Spirit, the Spirit of grace? We must come to trust the sanctifying Spirit that's at work inside us. Unlike legalism, grace-empowered holiness is not about trying to change our outward behavior to meet God's standard; rather, it starts with an internal transformation and works its way out toward behavior.

Clean the Inside

In one of His strongest rebukes, Jesus gave a warning to the Pharisees. *Woe to you, scribes and Pharisees, hypocrites! For you cleanse the outside of the cup and dish, but inside they are full of extortion and self-indulgence… first cleanse the inside of the cup and dish, that the outside of them may be clean also* (Matt 23:25-26). The religious system of the day focused on looking good. Jesus challenged this by saying that He was not nearly as concerned about the outside as He was the inside. We need this same challenge today in our behavior toward each other. If somebody's behavior doesn't match what we think is holiness, we are far too quick to judge their actions, instead of encouraging the grace of God at work in them.

We love our nation but in all of our lives, we've never seen it this divided. And neither side is holy, because holiness isn't the external; holiness comes from the heart. We can't watch any news channel without hearing people lie, distort, twist, and spin. So we all pick the one that we can best tolerate. Jesus help us! But it's not about externals; it is about having a clean heart. It's about the power of new covenant grace that forgives - and transforms.

But beware; we must not make the mistake of trying to find the balance between law and grace. Law and grace are incompatible; they come from two different trees. We must put our confidence completely in the grace of God, because Jesus fulfilled the law and then gave us His righteousness as a gift. So by grace, we can receive His righteousness and walk in the benefit of the gift we have received. That's not a liberty to sin, but a recipe for change. The true grace of God begins to work in the inside of us and changes both who we are and how we behave. If we'll connect grace and holiness correctly, then we will walk into ever-increasing freedom.

Highway of Holiness

And a highway shall be there, and a way; and it shall be called the Holy Way. The unclean shall not pass over it, but it shall be for the redeemed; the wayfaring men, yes, the simple ones and fools, shall not err in it and lose their way (Isa 35:8 AMP). Isaiah looks forward to the time when grace-empowered holiness will be released and calls it a highway of holiness. There's a narrow way to salvation, but the life of holiness is actually much wider than we've understood. When we talk about a highway, we think of a broad road easy to travel. But we also realize it has two ditches, the ditch on one side of the highway is legalism; the ditch on the other side is the misuse of grace that gives us license to sin. But the focus here is on the highway that we can walk on with confidence and security. The Holy Spirit at work in us is much more powerful than we realize.

We love the image of the highway, but we particularly

like the last phrase in the amplified, *the simple ones and fools, shall not err in it and lose their way.* Even when we behave foolishly on the highway, we won't get lost. That's the beauty of the power of grace. When we walk in grace-empowered holiness, we give people the liberty to mess up and yet stay in fellowship with each other. We give people the liberty to think contrary to what we think and still walk together. We give people the liberty to vote differently than we would vote and still love them. We get so uptight in our condemnation of people's actions instead of celebrating the grace of God at work in the lives of people.

We want to be a body of people that walks in grace-empowered holiness. Holiness so filled with grace that it changes the way we see the world around us. We want to be a body of people who see people through the eyes of God's grace at work and not through the eyes of our preferences, position, or ideology. We believe God is bringing us into a season of the highway, where holiness is no longer a treacherous mountain pass braved only by a few. We witness it in so many different places. There really is a highway of holiness that God has laid out in front of us. Give yourself the grace to change from the inside out. Give people around you the grace to change from the inside out, because a grace-empowered holiness will produce a lasting change.

External conformity will only produce a temporary solution. But if we will allow the Father to sneeze on us, we will catch a glorious virus. We will catch a holiness bug that settles down into the DNA of who we are and changes us from the inside out. We will be so transformed that we will naturally begin to represent Him to the world around us more accurately. So pray this with us:

Father, forgive us for seeking holiness from self-effort and from legalism that will never produce what we hunger to produce. Father, forgive us if we're allowing ourselves to do things that we know are not in line with Your holiness. Forgive us for any misuse, or abuse of Your grace. Father, right now we yield ourselves to Your Holy Spirit. We ask You to cause us to shift into a grace-empowered holiness that will transform us from the inside out. We choose to trust the causative power of Your grace at work in us.

4

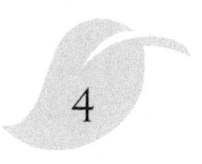

THE SPIRIT OF GRACE

What is the Holy Spirit's role in this life of grace?

The Holy Spirit is the causative and any study of grace would be incomplete without seeking to understand the role of the Spirit in the release and operation of grace. The writer of Hebrews refers to the Holy Spirit as the Spirit of grace (Heb. 10:29) who works with us and in us, enabling us to live secure in God's abundant grace. The precious gift of the Holy Spirit makes a life of grace possible.

When the Holy Spirit is invited into us as believers, the grace of God begins its transforming work. The resulting metamorphous is a proof of grace, meaning that the world around us begins to see a clearer representation of God's nature. This has nothing to do with our ability and everything to do with grace at work by the Spirit. It is the ministry of the Holy Spirit to administer God's grace.

The Holy Spirit functions as the revealer of Jesus. He literally divulges what Jesus is like and shows us how He thinks, how He feels and how He acts. John quotes Jesus as He spoke of the role of the Holy Spirit; *He will glorify me for He will take of mine and disclose it to you* (Jn. 16:14). The Holy Spirit doesn't speak on His own; He speaks and reveals what He hears from and sees in Jesus.

Through our lives, the Holy Spirit touches the hearts and lives of people around us and models the life of Jesus to them. They see Him patterned and fleshed out in us. "*Charis*" is the Greek word for grace. When the "*ma*" suffix is added it becomes *charisma*, which means either the result of grace or the proof of grace. Paul used this word for the gifts of the Spirit, which means that the activities of the Spirit flowing through us are the result of grace. Our ability to operate in the gifts of the Spirit provides proof of God's grace at work.

The Holy Spirit reveals Jesus to us and shows us how His nature and activity can be fleshed out in our life. Jesus calls the Holy Spirit the Spirit of Truth and says, …*He will testify regarding Me*. The word "testify" used here means, to give information based on personal knowledge. I remember buying our son a toolbox for his fifth birthday (of course it included one tool that I really needed). And now I'm the kind of grandpa that buys a train set for a one-year-old because I like to play with trains. He shows us how to play with a train set even if we don't appear old enough or mature enough. The Holy Spirit shows us how to use gifts that appear so much bigger than we are. He gives us access to the resources Jesus had and offers to teach us how to use anything He makes available.

When did we last see a resurrection from the dead? That forgotten tool lies dormant in the church's toolbox. We may not know how to use it yet, but we know Someone who will teach us how to use it when the time comes. We must understand that the Holy Spirit takes responsibility to reveal all we need so we can boldly step out in faith any time He asks. If we start to step out too early or too far, the Holy Spirit gently restrains us. If we will listen and respond, we will begin to see more than we could ever imagine.

It will be Better

Jesus makes a stunning statement about the Holy Spirit when He told the disciples that it was to their advantage for Him to leave (Jn. 16:7). He had just told his disciples, *without me you can do nothing* (Jn. 15:5), then He shocks them with, "And by the way, I'm going away, but it will be better for you after I'm gone." We can imagine the disciples' confusion. We're sure they thought, What are You talking about? You just said we couldn't do this without You and now You say You are leaving; how can we possibly be better off?

Looking back, we can see they were better off because the Holy Spirit could now individually direct the members of His body. Christ in His physical body could deal with an individual, but the omnipresent Holy Spirit could interact with every individual revealing the nature and words of Christ. There would be a new corporateness at work through the presence of the Holy Spirit. The presence of the life of Jesus would touch everyone who opens himself or herself to this work of grace.

If grace is the power of God at work changing us, then the Holy Spirit is the agent of that change. We must understand this crucial role of the Holy Spirit. The Holy Spirit never operates in isolation; He speaks only what He hears Jesus saying so that the words we speak accurately reflect the nature of Jesus. When Jesus describes the work of the Holy Spirit He says, *He will not speak on His own initiative, but whatever He hears, He will speak; and He will disclose to you what is to come. He shall glorify Me; for He shall take of Mine, and shall disclose it to you* (John 16:13,14).

As good charismatics, we focus a lot on our relationship with the Holy Spirit. It's not an overemphasis on the Spirit; rather, it's because through life in the Spirit, Jesus is honored. The Holy Spirit acts as the agent of Jesus. Agents have the responsibility to represent the owner and have the authority to act on the owner's behalf. The Holy Spirit as the agent of Jesus doesn't act from His own initiative. He operates with the instructions He's given by Jesus.

An agent has the responsibility of explaining the benefits. If we go to an agent of a company, it's their job to tell us all about the company and to describe the benefits we would receive if we did business with the company. The Holy Spirit explains the benefits to us. He literally tells us what Jesus has in store for us; that's His role. He speaks only what Jesus says, so He doesn't initiate communication; He only speaks what he hears.

Finally, an agent makes no independent decisions. The Holy Spirit doesn't decide to do something separate from Jesus. They are one. What an awesome mystery; the Godhead made up of three persons and yet one. From this place of oneness, the Holy Spirit simply communicates what He hears and discloses to us the things that Jesus would say and do.

How will we grow to understand more of God's incredible gift of grace? Will we understand it from a few meetings? We'd like to think our preaching was that powerful, but in reality, we need the Spirit of Truth to help us understand. In order for us to push back the confusion and see with clarity this incredible gift of God, we need the Holy Spirit to help us. Jesus explained that *when He, the Spirit of truth, comes, He will guide you into all truth* (Jn. 16.13). Earlier, Jesus outlines three aspects of the truth the Spirit would reveal. He told the disciples that when the Holy Spirit comes He would convict the world of sin, of righteousness, and of judgment (Jn. 16.8).

These three works of the Holy Spirit are important for us to understand. With this initial announcement of what the Holy Spirit will would do for us, Jesus provides the framework for everything He will say later about the Spirit. These serve as pillars of truth that give a foundation from which everything else will make sense. Not only does He spell it out, but in the following verses, He amplifies each one to be sure that we really get what He means. We believe that we need to delve into these truths if we want to understand the measure of grace available to us.

What to Believe - Conviction

First, we read that *He convicts… because they do not believe* (Jn. 16:8, 9). The revelation the Holy Spirit gives here helps us to believe. The Holy Spirit convicts us because we need to grasp something we haven't understood or put into practice. So the issue is belief. It does matter what we believe because faith affects everything we do. It affects our behavior, it changes the way we interact, and influences every decision in our life. The focus of the Spirit's conviction is to cause people to believe in Jesus. Conviction has a purpose: it brings repentance not just to make us turn from something, but so that we turn to something. His intention in bringing conviction is not the feeling of remorse but a change in our beliefs.

The purpose of conviction is an encounter with His grace, which produces real change. Conviction comes as God touches our heart through the Holy Spirit, producing a change that causes us to be more like Jesus. Conviction comes as His gentle voice warns us that we're missing the mark and if we don't steady our hand and move towards the center, we will begin to tip out of grace and back into works.

Sin can be defined as missing the mark. The Holy Spirit shows us the bulls-eye in the target, the position from which we can best represent Jesus. He works to conform us to His image with the goal of causing people to believe in Jesus. The change of belief we experience moves us from trying to do it in our own effort to trusting His mercy and grace. The change of belief moves us from self-righteousness to His righteousness. The change of belief moves us away from self-effort so we can stand secure in what He has done. The change means we know that His grace is enough for us.

Conviction moves us forward. When we understand this, we will let the Holy Spirit do His work. We know His role is to change us, so we respond and allow Him to do His work. If we resist, we will tend to make multiple laps around the same issue, which seems an awful waste of time.

Our prayer through it all is that God would teach us everything we need to know in this, because we want to come out of it and get into the next lap. Whatever it is, we want to face the new set of challenges. We don't want to go over and over the same set of circumstances, never changing, never breaking out; God help us. It is His grace that will break us into the next season.

It's the convicting power of the Holy Spirit that keeps us aligned with grace so we can function in freedom. His convicting power transforms our belief system so that we can reach our full potential. If we change our belief, it will change the way we feel and it will change the way we respond. If we believe we will fail, there is a good possibility that we will. If, however, we believe we will succeed, it becomes much more likely that we will. What we believe does affect the way we live our life. God's intention in giving us the Holy Spirit is to change our belief so we can represent Him well.

Repentance

Repentance by definition implies a change of direction. If we repent of something as a response to the Holy Spirit's conviction, that act requires a course correction. We were headed one way, but now we turn and go in a different direction. Peter tells us to, *repent therefore and return* (Acts 3:19). Repent and return together, are the essential components of repentance. Repentance is our response to the Holy Spirit telling us we drifted off the bulls-eye and the return element is the need to pull back toward the center of the target. We need to pull away from whatever we're involved in; this applies to both thoughts and actions.

We find this returning aspect in the definition of the Greek word for repentance, *metanoeo*, which means to think differently. The Holy Spirit works in us guiding our thoughts so that we reconsider the thoughts we allow and the decisions we make. He helps us change our mind by quietly teaching us to think differently. The purpose of this process is to get us back to grace. We need grace for those who have criticized us, betrayed us, or for people we just don't enjoy being around. We need grace to walk away from compromising situations and even more grace for ourselves when we fail.

If we will attune ourself to the voice of the Holy Spirit, the Spirit will keep us centered on the grace of God. He will not let us get into works. He will help us avoid self-effort. He will spare us from trying to create our own salvation or depending on our own righteousness. He will keep us operating in the grace of God. He looks at Jesus and watches us, diligently keeping the two aligned. That's the convicting role of the Spirit of grace at work in our life.

Where to Look - Righteousness

The second truth the Spirit reveals relates to righteousness. *And concerning righteousness, because I go to the Father and you no longer see me* (Jn. 16:10). The issue here is what do we see? Because Jesus returned to the Father we're not going to see Him for a while. We won't be able to watch Him and pattern our life off what He does. So the Holy Spirit will have to help us see Him correctly. The Spirit will show us what to look at and where we should put our focus. Do we understand that what we look at affects how we live? Do we know that where we set our focus influences our ability to persevere? Jesus models this Himself.

Hebrews refers to this truth; *fixing our eyes on Jesus the author and perfecter of our faith who for the joy set before Him endured* (Heb. 12:2). We need to get this revelation down in our spirit. Where did He focus His eyes when He went to the cross? He set His eyes on the joy in front of Him. He endured the cross because He fixed His eyes in the right place. If Jesus needed to keep His eyes in that right place, how much more do we? When we get our eyes on our circumstances, and the challenges that surround us, we're focused on the wrong thing.

We find it far too easy to focus on the issues we face in our lives. Often our challenges fill our vision until it's all we can see. But the Spirit convicts us that our focus is off. He begins to do some convicting concerning righteousness. He will help us see things that we're not seeing otherwise. If righteousness means that which is right or correct, the Spirit helps us see people or situations rightly or correctly – that is, from Jesus' perspective. The primary role of the Holy Spirit is revealing Jesus to us. He literally shows us how Jesus thinks, how He acts, how He feels and how He behaves.

The Holy Spirit gives us the words to speak the moment we need them. The words He gives mirror the words of Jesus; we know they come from Him because the Spirit does not speak on His own initiative. He speaks what He hears, giving us confidence that the words that come out of our mouth under His direction are what Jesus would say in the situation. If we will trust the Holy Spirit, we will literally speak the words of Jesus. The Holy Spirit doesn't make it up as He goes along; He's committed to only say what He hears. So if we trust the Holy Spirit to speak through us, we're speaking life-giving words, which will change the atmosphere.

Finally, the Holy Spirit reveals the righteousness of Christ and confirms our true identity. In the first section we looked at Paul's discussion about the source of righteousness but it is good to be reminded. He desired to *be found in Him not having a righteousness of my own derived from the law, but that which is through faith in Christ, the righteousness which comes from God on the basis of faith* (Phil. 3:9). Paul didn't want to find himself trusting his own righteousness, but rather wanted to live in the good of Christ's perfect righteousness that he received by faith. He wanted his identity based in the righteousness that comes from what Jesus has done. This is exactly the same for us today; we want our righteousness to come from faith in what Jesus has done. How do we find that righteousness? The Holy Spirit convicts us of all Jesus has done and confirms our new identity purchased through His blood.

This identity has nothing to do with how well we have done; it has everything to do with how well Jesus did. The Roman church was told that by faith they could receive *an abundance of grace and the gift of righteousness* (Rom 5:17). Righteousness is a gift! How do we get righteous? For too long we have behaved like it came by keeping the law. We have believed it somehow related to our good behavior. But the Bible says that our righteousness is filthy rags. And because it is impossible for us to ever behave righteously enough to please Him, He gives us His righteousness in place of our junk; what a gift. He gives us His perfect obedience to the law in place of our failure. He gives us what we could never obtain through our efforts. His righteousness comes to us as a gift in the same way that He gives us His salvation as a gift.

Paul confirmed this truth to the Corinthian church when he wrote: *He made Him who knew no sin to be sin on our behalf that we might become the righteousness of God in Him* (2 Cor. 5:21). Where did our sin go? On Him! The Father asked Jesus, who had perfectly obeyed the law, to take the penalty of sin on our behalf. The Father literally put our sin on Him. And what did He give us in exchange? He gave us Christ's righteousness. What a great exchange, our sin for His righteousness. The Holy Spirit keeps us focused on the right thing. If we get up one morning feeling like a hopeless failure, the Holy Spirit whispers that you're a beauty in His eyes. You're clothed in His righteousness; you're acceptable to Him. Even if we don't feel like it, the Spirit confirms the power of grace to us.

It's the Holy Spirit's role to confirm our identity so that we can go about our day with confidence, knowing who we are in Christ. Our standing before Him is not determined by our performance; it's based on His gift, a gift of righteousness. The work of sanctification in us conforms us to His likeness. We are not just clothed in the righteousness of Christ, He made us righteous and the sanctifying work of the Holy

Spirit teaches us to live in the good of what we already have as a gift from Him. The Holy Spirit works to convince us of who we really are, to disclose to us our true identity so we can live our lives in obedience to the righteous gift that we've been given. We choose to live in obedience from a position of righteousness not because we're trying to attain it; that's the change, the repentance from dead works that must take place.

How to Overcome – Judgment

Jesus also told us that the Holy Spirit gives us a revelation of judgment, *because the ruler of this world has been judged* (Jn. 16:11). The issue here is overcoming. Jesus points out that the enemy is already defeated, judged, and condemned. The Holy Spirit will reveal this truth and teach us how to overcome. We don't overcome by living in fear of the enemy. We overcome by understanding that the enemy is already defeated. The many schemes he tries to work on us are nothing but lies. He does not have the right to do what he threatens, because we live protected by the blood of the Lord Jesus. He does not have a legal right to us. The Holy Spirit's role is to remind us that the enemy is already under our feet, because he is under the feet of Jesus, and we are in Him. When we get in the middle of a battle, the Holy Spirit will show us the chariots of the Lord around us. In the worst conflict of our life the Holy Spirit will hold our living hope in front of us to remind us that victory is sure. We've already overcome because of what Christ has done. The Spirit keeps that truth before us so that we can live from a position of victory, rather than trying to get the victory.

Most of the church is still trying to get a victory they already have. Shake off the lie, victory is ours; take it and live in it. Jesus promised us that the Holy Spirit would convince us of the truth of this victory. He will show us how to overcome by executing the full extent of Christ's triumph over the enemy, by reminding us that the enemy has been defeated, judged, and condemned. Then, we simply reinforce the victory that Christ has already won.

Jesus says of Himself, *the Son of Man appeared for this purpose, that He might destroy the works of the evil one* (1 Jn. 3:8). This was Jesus' job description. Christ's purpose was to overthrow any work, powers or dominions opposed to the Kingdom of God. As those who walk in grace, our role is to allow the Holy Spirit to give us constant conviction of the defeat of our enemy so that we never walk in fear of what he might do. Many still live in this kind of fear, but we must walk with absolute certainty that victory is sure. We've won because He won. We've read the end of the book and see the triumph of our King. It doesn't matter what we see around us. It doesn't matter what circumstances we face; there is victory in Him. The more we listen to the conviction of the Holy Spirit the more confident we will become.

How many of us have seen God do some wonderful things and then suddenly it looks like the enemy came in and stirred things up? The enemy's purpose was to get us focused on his schemes and away from God's wonderful promises. Too often when we see his lies we respond by bemoaning our plight and surrendering to the attack. Stop it! Stop looking at the charade and get our eyes back on the victory. That's what the Holy Spirit does when He convicts of judgment. The enemy stands judged and condemned already. We need to learn to live in the reality of this truth. We need to allow it to breathe life into us. The Holy Spirit reminds us of our right to impose Christ's victory.

A final verse to reinforce this truth reads; *but in all these things we overwhelmingly conquer through Him who loved us* (Rom. 8:37). How many things does "all" include? Is there any circumstance not included? Is there anything in our life that doesn't fit into the category of "all?" It says, all because He means all; it doesn't matter how dire our situation looks. Many feel like it works for everybody else, but it doesn't work for them. That's a lie. If we will just allow Him, the Holy Spirit will convince us that in all these things we can overwhelmingly conquer.

If this is not our experience, we need the Holy Spirit to help us. If we feel like we get to the brink and don't go through, we need the Holy Spirit to help us reinforce our victory. If in all these things we almost get breakthrough but got stopped just short, it is time to repent and accept that we've missed something of the work of grace that comes through the Holy Spirit. As the grace of God works in us we begin to understand that in <u>all</u> these things we can overwhelmingly conquer. We don't just win; we annihilate the schemes of the enemy.

God loved us so much that He sent His Son, giving us access to an indescribable gift of His grace. Through His grace, we live knowing we are loved and forgiven. We live secure in our identity because the Holy Spirit convinces us of the profound transforming effect of Christ's righteousness at work in us. He has overwhelmed us with His goodness and positioned us so that we can overwhelmingly conquer. Because of grace, when we stand in the face of the enemy there is no question about who wins, because we powerfully conquer. Let's not offend the Spirit of grace by trying to do this through our own effort. Surrender to the work of the precious Holy Spirit and let Him do His convicting work in us.

With the help of the Holy Spirit, we will start to live from victory to victory. We are promised that in all these things we can and will forcibly conquer. How many of us need to conquer some things? We can forcefully conquer because of the grace of God. We need to allow the Holy Spirit to reveal to us what Christ's grace has already accomplished so that we begin to overwhelming conquer. Take a stand, and allow the Holy Spirit to disclose the victory that is ours. Let Him convict us of victory. That word "convict" literally means to take the wraps off what is hidden and bring it into manifestation. Right now ask the Holy Spirit to bring the victory of Jesus into full manifestation in your life. Pray with us:

> *Lord Jesus we surrender to Your Lordship. We choose to live in our full identity by living and walking in fellowship and obedience to the Holy Spirit. We rejoice in our adoption as Sons and Daughters and rest secure in the Father's pleasure. We put our trust in Your indescribable grace and receive Your precious gift of Righteousness. From this moment we step into the identity You purchased for us with Your blood and out of our brokenness. Thank you Jesus for your amazing grace.*

Printed in Great Britain
by Amazon